Football

Written by Sue Barraclough
Photography by Chris Fairclough

W
FRANKLIN WATTS
LONDON • SYDNEY

First published in 2006 by Franklin Watts
338 Euston Road, London NW1 3BH

Franklin Watts Australia
Hachette Children's Books
Level 17/207 Kent Street
Sydney NSW 2000

Editor: Adrian Cole
Designer: Jemima Lumley
Art direction: Jonathan Hair
Photography: Chris Fairclough, except pages 3, 16, 17, 28 and 29

The publisher wishes to thank all the staff and players at Bristol
City Football Club for their help in the production of this book.
Photographs on pages 3, 16, 17, 28 and 29 © Joe Meredith.

A CIP catalogue record for this book is available
from the British Library

ISBN 0 7496 6392 8

Dewey decimal classification number: 796.334

Printed in China

Contents

I am a footballer

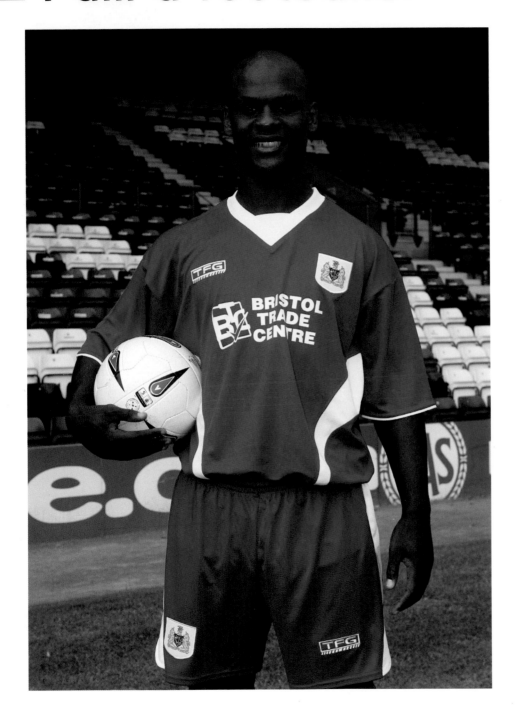

My name is Leroy. I am a striker in a football team. I spend most of my time training. It makes me fit so I can play well.

I train with the rest of the team nearly
every day. This helps all of us play
well together during football matches.

Training in the gym

A normal day starts with exercise in the gym.
We use equipment to warm up slowly.

We use weights to make us strong.
Exercise is part of our training. It keeps us fit.

At the training ground

After the gym, we go to the training ground. It has four pitches and equipment to help us practise.

We do
different
jumping,
stepping
and running
exercises.

Scoring skills

I am a striker so it is my job to score goals. The coach helps me and the other strikers to improve our scoring skills.

I need to run fast, kick strongly and turn quickly.

At the stadium

We play matches at our stadium.
The ground staff make sure the grass
on the pitch is cut. It needs to be
ready for the match at the weekend.

RLING ATYEO STAND
Take the gamble out of
computer network support
flybe.com
LEGAL PROTECTION
sky

Playing in a match

We play matches against other teams. Sometimes we play in our stadium and sometimes we play in another team's stadium.

All my training helps me to work hard and score goals. I love to score goals and to hear the crowd cheer my name.

Drinking and eating

During matches and training it is important to drink water. There are always water bottles to use.

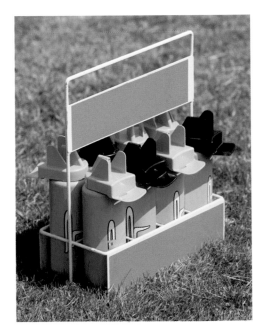

I eat a healthy lunch every day.
It gives me the energy to play football.

Practice match

As part of our training we divide into two teams and play a practice match. We wear blue or yellow shirts to show which side we are on.

I am on the blue team. The teams warm
up and then we start the match.

Controlling the ball

Playing a practice match is a good way to improve all of our skills at controlling the ball.

I need to win control of the ball, pass by the defenders and then try to score a goal.

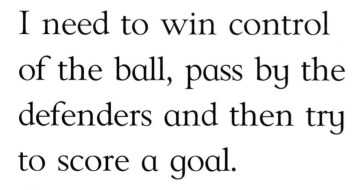

End of training

We worked hard during the practice match. Now we all need lots of water to drink and to help cool down.

It is time to pack up our gear and go back to the stadium for a shower. We will be training again tomorrow for our next match.

Football equipment

A **football strip** is made in the football club's colours. The strip helps the players on the pitch to see who is on each team. Fans wear the team colours, too.

Football boots are important. They are very lightweight and have studs underneath to help the players run on grass.

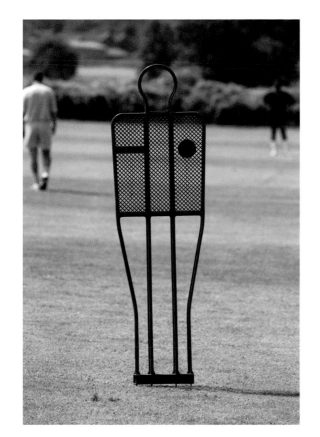

Dummy players can be stuck into the ground on the training pitch. They are pretend players on another team. Dummy players are used to practise team play and passing skills.

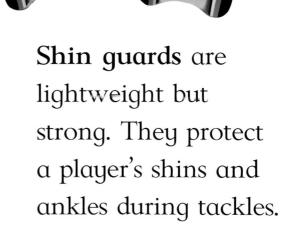

A **football** is made up of leather pieces stitched together. It is waterproof and hard wearing.

Shin guards are lightweight but strong. They protect a player's shins and ankles during tackles.

Becoming a footballer

Leroy started playing football when he was 10 years old. He played for Chelsea Football Club's Youth Team when he was about 13. At 17 he moved to Bristol City Football Club on a three-year training scheme with a scholarship. Leroy was signed up as a professional when he was 18. He played for the England under-21 team at 20. Now he plays football for Reading Football Club.

To be a top footballer you need:

- To play well as part of a team.
- To be healthy, fit, fast and agile.
- To learn excellent ball control, passing and shooting skills.
- To listen to advice from the coach and accept decisions.

Glossary and index